Contents

Some words are shown in bold, **like this**. You can find out what they mean by looking in the Glossary.

What happens to the food I eat?

Do you know what happens to food after you chew it and swallow it? First, it travels down your throat. Then it goes through a pipe called the **oesophagus** (ih-sah-fah-gus), and into your stomach. From there, it moves through a long, tube-like **organ** called the small intestine. As it moves, the food is broken down more and more.

The food's **nutrients** are taken in through your intestine walls. Those nutrients give your body energy and help it grow. This is called **digestion**.

BODY FACT

The best way to get all the nutrients your body needs is to eat plenty of vegetables and fruits.

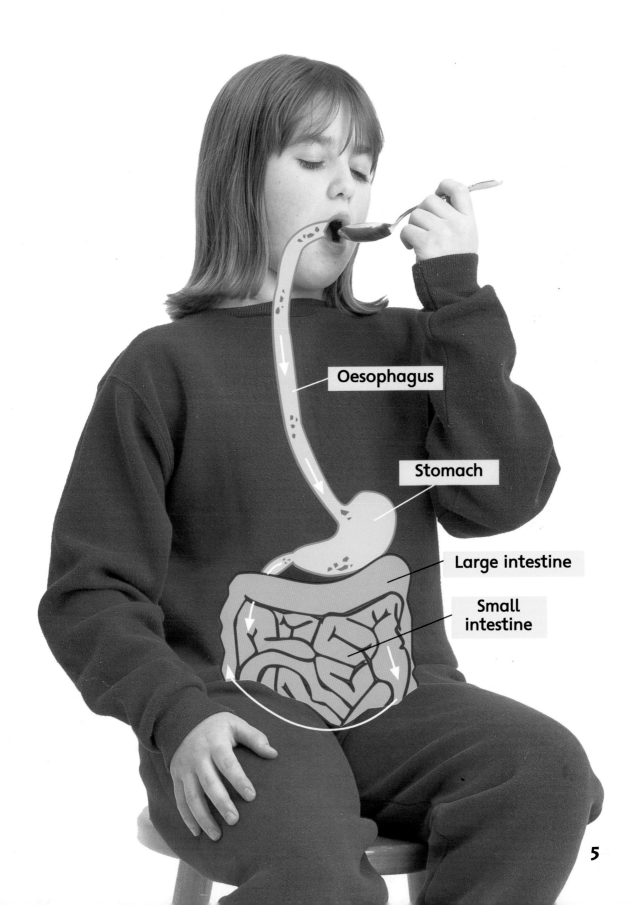

Oesophagus

Stomach

Large intestine

Small intestine

5

How do I digest food?

Digestion really begins when you start chewing. As you chew, the liquid in your mouth, called **saliva,** starts to break down food. In your stomach, other liquids break down the food even more. From your stomach, food passes into your small intestine.

Inside the small intestine, food is broken down into smaller bits. These bits are so tiny they can pass from the small intestine right into your blood vessels.

Some food cannot be digested. It passes into the large intestine. Your body then gets rid of this leftover food, or waste, through the **anus**.

BODY FACT

After you eat a meal, try to choose a quiet activity to do. This will help you to digest your food.

Why do I feel hungry?

Air moving around in your stomach causes rumbling that you can hear. ("Tummy" and "stomach" mean the same thing.)

BODY FACT

Food usually stays in your stomach for three to four hours. That's why you need to eat a meal or snack about every four hours during the day.

1 Your stomach and your intestines move all the time.

2 When all the food is gone from your stomach or intestines, air fills those parts of your body.

3 As muscles in your stomach and intestines move the air around, the moving air makes a rumbling sound.

4 Then your tummy rumbles, and you know you're hungry!

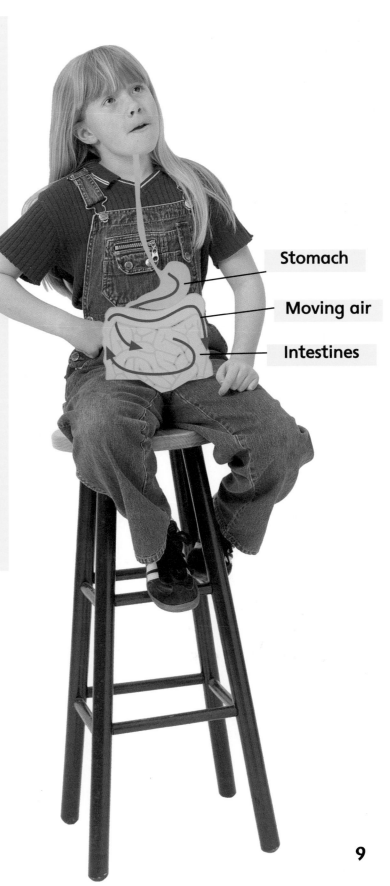

Stomach

Moving air

Intestines

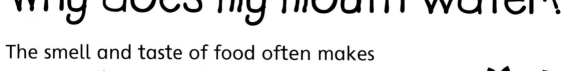

Why does my mouth water?

The smell and taste of food often makes your mouth water with **saliva**.

1 The smell of food reaches your brain.

2 Your brain sends a message to your salivary **glands** telling them to produce saliva.

3 Once you begin to eat, chewing causes more saliva to be produced.

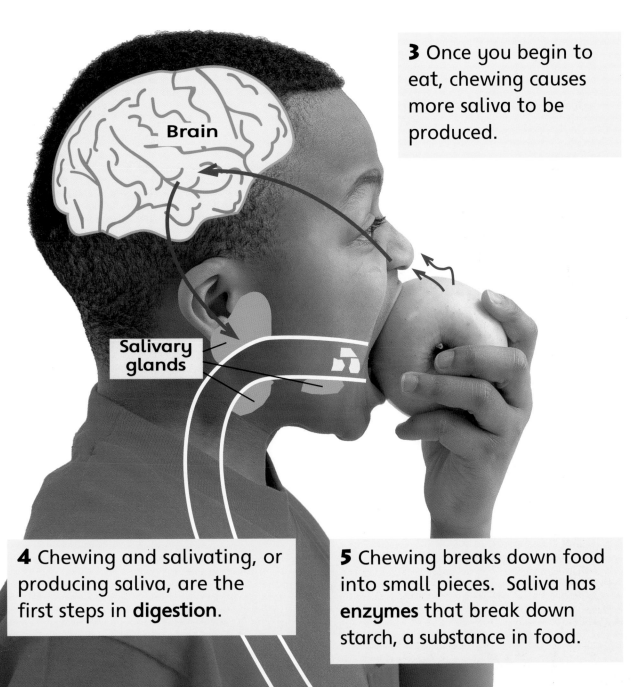

Brain

Salivary glands

4 Chewing and salivating, or producing saliva, are the first steps in **digestion**.

5 Chewing breaks down food into small pieces. Saliva has **enzymes** that break down starch, a substance in food.

What is a burp?

Air travelling up through your **oesophagus** comes out of your mouth in a burp.

BODY FACT

Burps help you digest food and feel more comfortable.

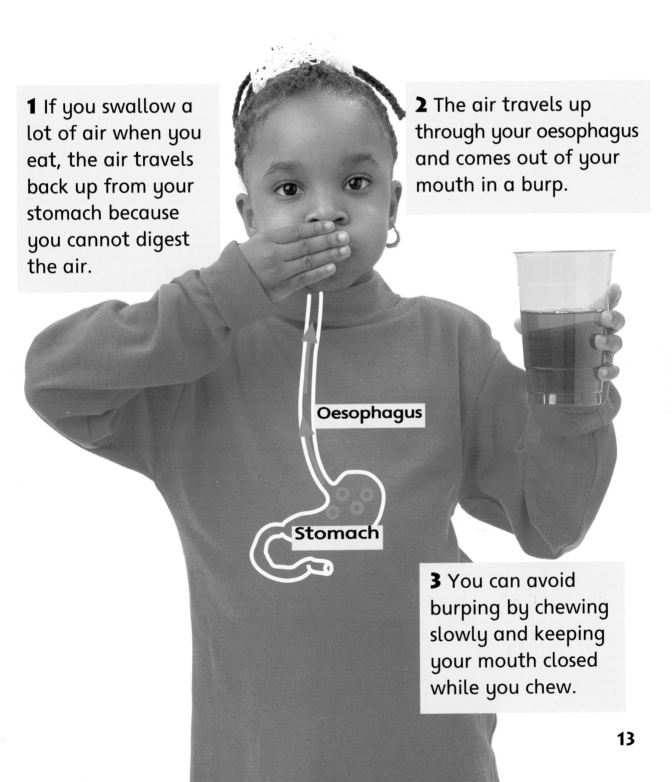

1 If you swallow a lot of air when you eat, the air travels back up from your stomach because you cannot digest the air.

2 The air travels up through your oesophagus and comes out of your mouth in a burp.

Oesophagus

Stomach

3 You can avoid burping by chewing slowly and keeping your mouth closed while you chew.

Why do I get a tummy ache when I eat too much?

The squeezing of muscles in your stomach gives you a tummy ache.

BODY FACT

Fatty foods like chips and ice cream are hard for your body to digest. If you eat meals that don't have too many fatty foods, you will feel better.

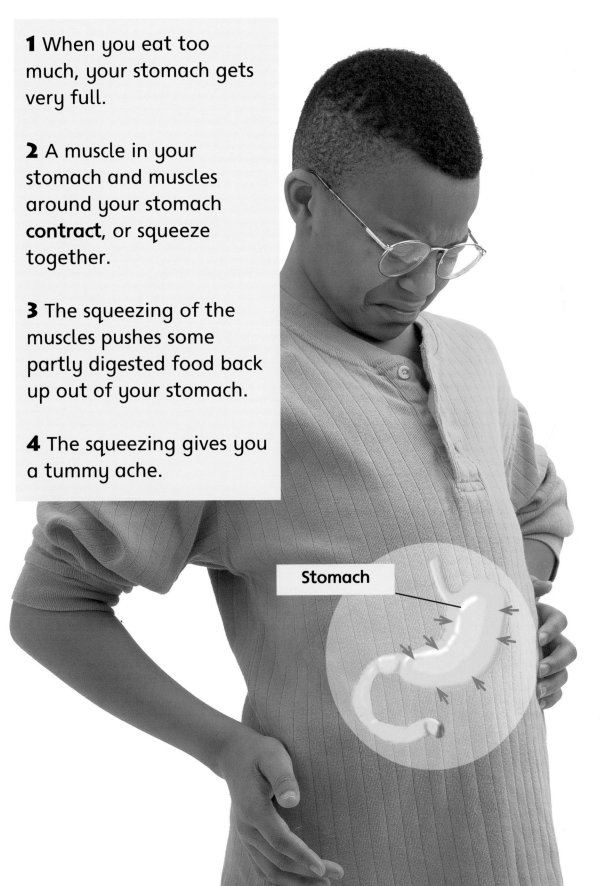

1 When you eat too much, your stomach gets very full.

2 A muscle in your stomach and muscles around your stomach **contract**, or squeeze together.

3 The squeezing of the muscles pushes some partly digested food back up out of your stomach.

4 The squeezing gives you a tummy ache.

Stomach

Why do I vomit?

A large muscle near your stomach works with the muscles in your **abdomen** to squeeze partly digested food up out of your stomach. The food travels up your **oesophagus**, and out your mouth.

BODY FACT
Vomiting can help your body get rid of something harmful, such as food that is off.

1 Maybe you've eaten or drunk too much too fast. A lot of partly digested food or liquid in your stomach can make you vomit.

2 When you have too much partly digested food in your stomach, it sends a message to a special part of your brain.

3 Your brain sends a message to your stomach that there is too much partly digested food in your stomach.

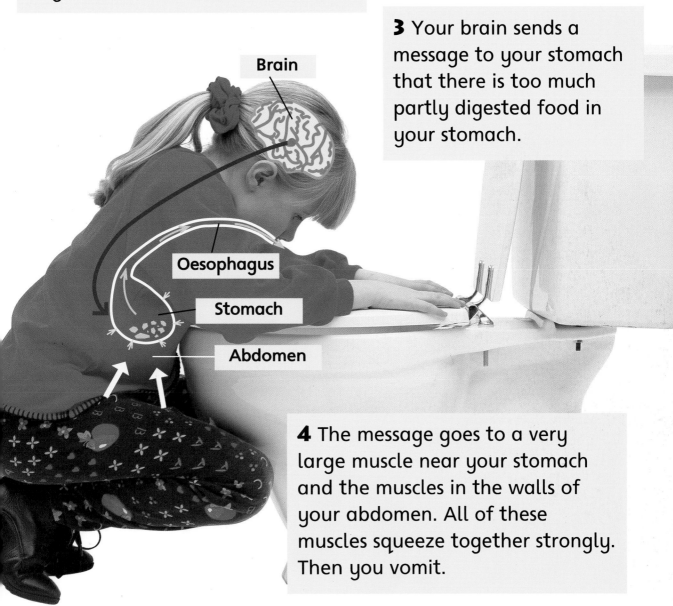

Brain

Oesophagus

Stomach

Abdomen

4 The message goes to a very large muscle near your stomach and the muscles in the walls of your abdomen. All of these muscles squeeze together strongly. Then you vomit.

Why do I pass wind?

Bacteria in your large intestine help break down food. The bacteria and partly broken down food can sometimes produce **gas**.

BODY FACT

Many foods that may produce a lot of gas are very healthy. Examples are apples, broccoli and onions.

● You have millions of bacteria in your body. Bacteria are tiny living things that you can't see. Some bacteria are harmful. Others are helpful.

● Helpful bacteria in your large intestine help break down food.

● As the bacteria break down food, gas is sometimes produced.

● When some foods, like beans, are broken down in the large intestine, a large amount of gas is produced.

● When a lot of gas builds up, it comes out through the **anus,** the opening at the end of the large intestine.

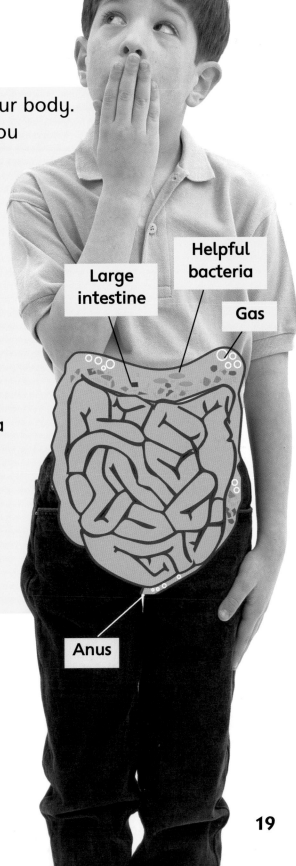

Large intestine

Helpful bacteria

Gas

Anus

19

Why do I go to the toilet?

You go to the toilet so that your body can get rid of liquid and solid waste.

BODY FACT
After you eat, it takes an average of 24 hours for **nutrients** to be absorbed by the small intestine.

1 Liquids and solids that cannot be digested go from your small intestine to your large intestine.

Large intestine

Small intestine

Kidneys

2 The liquid passes into your blood vessels through the walls of the large intestine. Then the liquid is taken out of your blood by a pair of **organs** called your kidneys.

Bladder

3 Next, the water goes to a bag-like organ called a bladder. Then it passes out of your body as **urine**.

Anus

4 Undigested solid food is called **faeces**. It comes out of your large intestine through your **anus**.

Explore more!
Your digestive system

1 MOUTH-WATERING MADNESS!

WHAT YOU'LL NEED:

• A handkerchief or something to use as a blindfold
• Two of your favourite foods
• One food you don't like
• A friend to help you

THEN TRY THIS!

Have your friend blindfold you. Then, one at a time, your friend should hold up a food for you to smell. Take a deep sniff. See if you salivate after smelling each food. Can you tell which foods made your mouth water the most? Did some foods not make your mouth water at all?

3 BUBBLY BURPS

WHAT YOU'LL NEED:
- Juice or water
- A fizzy drink

THEN TRY THIS!

Take a few gulps of juice or water. Do you feel a burp inside? Then take a few gulps of something fizzy. Feel the air inside create a burp. You can let it out in a great big BURP!

2 ARE YOU A TRUE-BLUE CHEWER?

WHAT YOU'LL NEED:
- Some bread to chew.

THEN TRY THIS!

Take a big bite of bread and chew it without swallowing. Keep chewing and chewing. Soon the bread will start to taste sweet. This is because an **enzyme** in your **saliva** turns the starch in bread into sugar.

...e part of your body
...tween the bottom of your
chest and your hips

anus – the opening at the end of
the large intestine

bacteria – tiny living things that
are all around you and also
inside your body

contract – to make smaller by
squeezing together

digestion – the breaking down of
food into tiny parts

enzymes – substances in your
body that help break down
food

faeces – undigested solid food
that passes out of your body
through your **anus**

glands – organs that make
materials for the body to use

nutrients – the things in food
that keep you healthy and help
you grow

oesophagus – the tube that
carries food from the throat to
the stomach

organ – a part of the body that
does one job

saliva – liquid released by the
glands in your mouth that
begins the breakdown of food

urine – liquid waste taken out of
your body by the kidneys

24

Index